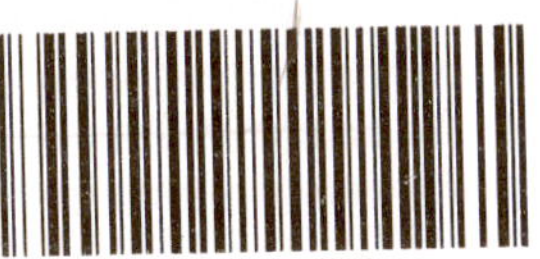

Let all that you do be done in

LOVE.

1 Corinthians 16:14

927-3902

This Book Belongs to

____

Gift From

____

Date

____

THE SECRET POWER OF SPEAKING GOD'S WORD

Joyce Meyer

Printed in the United States of America.

First Printing, 2019

ISBN : 978-1-942854-95-1

Joyce Meyer Ministries
P.O. Box 655
Fenton, Missouri 63026
joycemeyer.org

CONTENTS

A NOTE FROM JOYCE

Did you know what you're holding in your hands isn't an ordinary book? This little purple book is filled with God's promises that you can speak out loud over your life, and help you get to know God and understand Him better each time you open it up.

Proverbs 7:2-3 tells us, *...Keep my teaching as the apple of your eye...write them on the tablet of your heart.* God wants you to know His Word deep in your heart so that you will always remember, and never forget, His love for you and the wonderful plans He has for you! I want to encourage you to say a little bit of God's Word out loud each day, just like you wash your face, brush your teeth and fix your hair.

You can keep this book under your pillow and read it at night or in the morning when you wake up. You can put it in your backpack and share it with friends at school.

You can even set aside a special time to read it with your mom, dad or any of the special people in your life!

The more you say God's Word out loud, the more you will know what's right from wrong, what's true and false, and what this journey called life is all about. Little by little, you'll become stronger, braver, kinder and more loving because you'll have His Word working inside of you!

I pray that this book will help you know and understand how loved and treasured you are by God. He loves you more than anything, and He wants you to know about the special purpose you have in His family and the wonderful adventures He has planned for your life!

Love you,

Joyce Meyer

SPEAKING GOD'S WORD ABOUT...

BEING KIND

Kindness is a way of treating people that makes them feel special and loved. It's the way you want to be treated yourself. You can share kindness with anyone—and there are so many ways to do it! You can tell your friend something nice, share your toys with your brother, let someone go first when it's your turn, or help your mom clean up a mess. Kindness is a gift from God—and He wants us to share His gifts with everyone.

Let all that you do be done in love.
I Corinthians 16:14

I do everything with love.

—

Kind words are like honey—sweet to the soul and healthy for the body. Proverbs 16:24 NLT

I say nice things to others and it makes them feel great.

—

But the fruit of the Spirit is love, joy, peace, patience, kindness, goodness, faithfulness, gentleness, self-control; against such things there is no law. Galatians 5:22-23

God has given me everything I need to be like Him - things like His love, joy, peace, patience, kindness, goodness, faithfulness, gentleness, and self-control.

—

Do to others as you would have them do to you. Luke 6:31 NIV

I treat others the way I want to be treated.

—

And the Lord's servant must not be quarrelsome but kind to everyone.... 2 Timothy 2:24

Because I serve God, I don't argue with people. I am kind to everyone.

Whoever pursues righteousness and kindness will find life, righteousness, and honor. Proverbs 21:21

When I am good and truthful and kind, I have joy and peace and I know I've done a great job.

—

Therefore encourage one another and build one another up, just as you are doing.
I Thessalonians 5:11

I am good at encouraging others and I will keep on doing it.

—

Put on then, as God's chosen ones, holy and beloved, compassionate hearts, kindness, humility, meekness, and patience, bearing with one another.... Colossians 3:12-13

God chose me, and I choose to be like Him. That means I will be kind, patient and put others first.

Strive for peace with everyone, and for the holiness without which no one will see the Lord. Hebrews 12:14

I try to be peaceful with everyone and to love God with all my heart.

DOING THE RIGHT THING

God lets us make our own choices and we have plenty to make. Sometimes they are small decisions like; *Should I spend my money on candy or save up for something better*? Other times they are big decisions like; *Should I lie about doing my homework or should I tell the truth*? Our decisions matter more than you know! When you're not sure what to do, ask God to help you think them through.

...Blessed is the man who fears the Lord, who greatly delights in his commandments! Psalm 112:1

God always knows what to do, and I happily do what He says.

...I have set before you life and death, blessing and curse. Therefore choose life, that you and your offspring may live. Deuteronomy 30:19

God lets me choose between doing what's good for me and what's not good for me. And I choose to do the right thing.

—

Search me, O God, and know my heart! Try me and know my thoughts! And see if there be any grievous way in me, and lead me in the way everlasting! Psalm 139:23-24

God knows what's in my heart and what I'm thinking about. If I'm making the wrong choice, He will show me so I can do the right thing.

—

...He guides me along right paths, bringing honor to his name. Psalm 23:3 NLT

God looks out for me and leads me to do what's right.

...The Lord will withhold no good thing from those who do what is right. Psalm 84:11 NLT

If I keep on doing what's right, God will keep on showing me His goodness. He won't hold back!

—

And let us not grow weary of doing good, for in due season we will reap, if we do not give up. Galatians 6:9

I've been doing what God says is right and I'm not going to stop now.

—

The fear of the Lord is the beginning of wisdom.... Proverbs 9:10

The smartest thing I can do is listen to what God says.

Wisdom is more precious than rubies; nothing you desire can compare with her.
Proverbs 3:15 NLT

God's wisdom is the best gift ever. It's worth more than precious jewels like rubies.

FEAR

We all feel afraid sometimes. Even Jesus felt afraid. But when Jesus lives inside of you, you don't have to be scared because He is always with you. Maybe you're feeling afraid because you are going to a new school or you don't like being alone in the dark. Maybe it's because your mom or dad are gone for a night. Any time you start to feel afraid, all you have to do is ask Jesus to be with you and He can take that fear away!

Have I not commanded you? Be strong and courageous. Do not be frightened, and do not be dismayed, for the Lord your God is with you wherever you go. Joshua 1:9

I am strong and brave because God is always with me.

The Lord is my light and my salvation; whom shall I fear? The Lord is the stronghold of my life; of whom shall I be afraid? Psalm 27:1

God brings light to dark places and helps me not be afraid.

—

Wait for the Lord; be strong, and let your heart take courage; wait for the Lord! Psalm 27:14

God is coming to help me. I'm waiting for Him!

—

When I am afraid, I put my trust in you. Psalm 56:3

When I'm afraid, I will count on Jesus to be there for me.

—

Even though I walk through the valley of the shadow of death I will fear no evil, for you are

with me; your rod and your staff, they comfort me. Psalm 23:4

Even when things are hard, God is with me and makes me feel better.

—

Don't be afraid, for I am with you. Don't be discouraged, for I am your God. I will strengthen you and help you. I will hold you up with my victorious right hand. Isaiah 41:10 NLT

I do not have to be afraid because God is with me and He is on my side and He makes me strong.

—

For God has not given us a spirit of fear and timidity, but of power, love, and self-discipline. 2 Timothy 1:7 NLT

Fear doesn't come from God. He gives me His strength, love and helps me to think before I act.

Be strong, and let your heart take courage, all you who wait for the Lord. Psalm 31:24

God is coming to help me. I'm sure of it!

—

I prayed to the Lord, and he answered me. He freed me from all my fears. Psalm 34:4 NLT

God hears my prayers and He takes away all my fears.

FEELING SAD

We all feel sad sometimes, but God is really good at making us feel better. He cares for us, and He loves to see us laugh and smile! So, when you fall down and get hurt, or when you feel like no one listens to you or understands, or when your heart feels broken, you can run to God and talk to Him about it. He'll fix you right up! God is your best friend, and you can tell Him anything.

The Lord is near to the brokenhearted and saves the crushed in spirit. Psalm 34:18

When my heart hurts, God is here with me. He takes away my sadness.

—

Jesus wept. John 11:35

Jesus cried too. He knows how I feel.

Trust in him at all times, you people; pour out your hearts to him, for God is our refuge. Psalm 62:8 NIV

I can always trust God with my true feelings, so I tell Him everything! He is my safe place.

—

You keep track of all my sorrows. You have collected all my tears in your bottle. You have recorded each one in your book. Psalm 56:8 NLT

God knows when I'm sad and when I've been crying. My tears matter to God. He knows what I'm going through, and He will take care of me.

—

Those who look to him are radiant, and their faces shall never be ashamed. Psalm 34:5

Thinking about God fills my heart with joy, and my face shows it!

Whom have I in heaven but you? And there is nothing on earth that I desire besides you. My flesh and my heart may fail, but God is the strength of my heart and my portion forever. Psalm 73:25-26

God is everything to me! Nothing else on earth could take His place in my heart. When I feel weak, He makes me strong! He is all I will ever need.

—

See, I have engraved you on the palms of my hands; your walls are ever before me. Isaiah 49:16 NIV

God is always thinking of me. He even etched me on the palms of His hands!

—

As a mother comforts her child, so will I comfort you" Isaiah 66:13 NIV

Just like moms comfort their babies, God holds me in His arms until I'm better.

Praise be to the God and Father of our Lord Jesus Christ, the Father of compassion and the God of all comfort, who comforts us in all our troubles, so that we can comfort those in any trouble with the comfort we ourselves receive from God. 2 Corinthians 1:3-4 NIV

God comforts me all the time. So, when somebody else is hurting, I know how to help them.

FOLLOWING GOD

The Bible tells us all about God's love for us and all the cool things He wants to help us do. From the very beginning of the book, we learn that God made us and He wants to be a big part of our lives. He knows we won't do everything perfectly. You see, God didn't make us robots. But He wants us to choose for ourselves whether or not we will love Him in return, and follow His Word.

For God called you to do good, even if it means suffering, just as Christ suffered for you. He is your example, and you must follow in his steps. He never sinned, nor ever deceived anyone. He did not retaliate when he was insulted, nor threaten revenge when he suffered. He left his case in the hands of God, who always judges fairly. I Peter 2:21-23 NLT

I'll try to be like Jesus—I won't lie, I'll try not to sin, and I won't get mad easily.

—

Jesus said to him, "I am the way, and the truth, and the life. No one comes to the Father except through me. John 14:6

Jesus doesn't just know the way...He is the way! He is the only way to God.

—

...He guides me along right paths, bringing honor to his name. Psalm 23:3 NLT

God gives me good directions.

—

I will always obey your law, for ever and ever. I will walk about in freedom, for I have sought out your precepts. Psalm 119:44-45 NIV

I will obey God's Word forever! Then I can be who He made me to be.

...This is God, our God forever and ever. He will guide us forever. Psalm 48:14

God is always with me and I will follow Him and listen to Him forever!

—

You have charged us to keep your commandments carefully. Psalm 119:4 NLT

I am careful to do what God asks.

—

Your word is a lamp to my feet and a light to my path. Psalm 119:105

God's Word leads me. It keeps me from stumbling around in the dark.

—

...Be steadfast, immovable, always abounding in the work of the Lord, knowing that in the Lord your labor is not in vain. I Corinthians 15:58

I'm doing things God's Way no matter what, and someday I'll be glad I did.

—

Do not merely listen to the Word...Do what it says. James 1:22 NIV

I don't just listen to God's Word, I do what it says.

—

"Do not follow the crowd in doing wrong...." Exodus 23:2

Even when my friends are doing the wrong thing, I choose to do what's right.

FORGIVING & SAYING SORRY

Everybody makes mistakes. And we all need to say "I'm sorry" sometimes. God says that when we hurt someone else's feelings, we're really hurting Him. But God is always quick to forgive us when we apologize, and He wants us to forgive ourselves quickly too...and then try to do the right thing next time. God also asks us to do the same thing and forgive other people when they hurt our feelings. He teaches us to love people perfectly, just like He does.

For all have sinned and fall short of the glory of God, and are justified by his grace....
Romans 3:23-24

Even though I have sinned and made mistakes, God always helps me make things right.

There is therefore now no condemnation for those who are in Christ Jesus. Romans 8:1

After I say "I'm sorry," I don't have to think about my mistakes anymore because of what Jesus did for me.

—

...your sins are forgiven for his name's sake. I John 2:12

I am forgiven because of what Jesus did for me.

—

So if the Son sets you free, you will be free indeed. John 8:36

God forgives me so I can forget my mistakes and love my life every day!

—

...As the Lord has forgiven you, so you also must forgive. Colossians 3:13

Just like God forgives me, when someone hurts me, I need to forgive them.

For if you forgive others their trespasses, your heavenly Father will also forgive you, but if you do not forgive others their trespasses, neither will your Father forgive your trespasses. Matthew 6:14-15

I forgive others and God forgives me.

—

"And whenever you stand praying, forgive, if you have anything against anyone, so that your Father also who is in heaven may forgive you your trespasses." Mark 11:25-26

When I'm talking to God, I will ask Him to help me forgive my friends, and when I mess up, I will say "I'm sorry."

—

Be kind to one another, tenderhearted, forgiving one another, as God in Christ forgave you. Ephesians 4:32

I am kind toward others, and quick to say "I'm sorry," and forgive them too.

GOD ALWAYS COMES THROUGH

Have you ever wondered: Is God listening to my prayers? Or, When is He ever going to come help me? Lots of us can feel that way when we're waiting to see the answers to our prayers. Sometimes we have to wait a long, long time, but God ALWAYS hears us and has a good reason for the wait. He knows what's best for us! And what He wants you to know down deep in your heart is that if you put your hope in Him, He will always come through. And when He does, you'll have so much fun telling your friends about the amazing thing God did for you.

Behold, the eye of the Lord is on those who fear him, on those who hope in his steadfast love.
Psalm 33:18

God knows that I trust Him, and He's looking out for me!

—

Hope deferred makes the heart sick, but a desire fulfilled is a tree of life. Proverbs 13:12

It hurts to wait sometimes, but when God answers my prayers it feels wonderful!

—

"The Lord is my portion," says my soul, "therefore I will hope in him." Lamentations 3:24

God gives me everything I need. He never lets me down.

—

May the God of hope fill you with all joy and peace in believing, so that by the power of the Holy Spirit you may abound in hope. Romans 15:13

God fills me with so much peace and joy when I trust Him. I am overflowing with hope!

Having hope will give you courage. You will be protected and will rest in safety. You will lie down unafraid, and many will look to you for help. Job 11:18-19 NLT

Hope gives me courage—and God protects me. I don't have to be afraid, and I can help others be unafraid too!

—

Rejoice in hope, be patient in tribulation, be constant in prayer. Romans 12:12

Hope makes me happy! I am peaceful even when life is hard and I have to be patient. I pray all the time.

—

For everything that was written in the past was written to teach us, so that through the endurance taught in the Scriptures and the encouragement they provide we might have hope. Romans 15:4 NIV

The Bible teaches me how to live my life. It makes me strong, encourages me and gives me hope.

"...In this world you will have trouble. But take heart! I have overcome the world." John 16:33 NIV

When I have a problem, I talk to God about it. He makes everything better because He is a big God!

—

Be strong and take heart, all you who hope in the Lord. Psalm 31:24 NIV

I can be strong and trust in God. My confidence in Him grows stronger every day!

—

Jesus Christ is the same yesterday and today and forever. Hebrews 13:8

Jesus is always, always, always the same!

GOD IS A BIG GOD!

No one can say how big and strong and powerful God is...but it sure is fun to think about! The Bible says He made the whole world in six days! He placed the sun, moon and stars in the sky. He parted the waters of the Red Sea, so His people could go free...and He can move a mountain if you really need Him to. God is so strong and powerful that nothing on earth or in Heaven can ever stand against Him.

Yours, O Lord, is the greatness and the power and the glory and the victory and the majesty, for all that is in the heavens and in the earth is yours.... I Chronicles 29:11

God made everything, and it all belongs to Him.

God saw all that he had made, and it was very good...Thus the heavens and the earth were completed in all their vast array.
Genesis 1:31, 2:1 NIV

Everything God makes is good! From all the birds to the plants and animals that live on the earth and in the sea...and even me!

—

...I am the Lord, and there is no other. I form light and create darkness; I make well-being and create calamity; I am the Lord, who does all these things. Isaiah 45:6-7

God is the only God. He made daytime and night time. He knows what He's doing.

—

...He will not grow tired or weary, and his understanding no one can fathom. Isaiah 40:28 NIV

God never gets tired. He never has to go to sleep. And no one is as smart as He is.

With a mighty hand and outstretched arm; His love endures forever. Psalm 136:12 NIV

God's love for me never runs out. It goes on forever!

—

..."Look! The Lamb of God who takes away the sin of the world! John 1:29 NLT

Jesus is God's Son, and He takes my sin away.

—

When I consider your heavens, the work of your fingers, the moon and the stars, which you have set in place, what is mankind that you are mindful of them, human beings that you care for them? Psalm 8:3-4 NIV

When I think about all that God has made...the moon and the stars...I feel so small! But God still cares for me.

GOD IS GOOD!

If there's one thing you should know about God, it's that He is good. The Bible tells us that God loves us more than anything—and that will never change. That means no matter what you do (or don't do), His love for you will always be the same. Plus, God wants you to enjoy each day of your life, and He has lots of fun adventures planned for you. All you have to do is what His Word tells you to do.

The Lord is good to all; he has compassion on all he has made. Psalm 145:9 NIV

God is good! He cares for me and everything He's made.

—

Give thanks to the Lord, for he is good. His love endures forever. Psalm 136:1 NIV

I thank God! He is good, and His love goes on forever.

The steadfast love of the Lord never ceases; his mercies never come to an end; they are new every morning; great is your faithfulness. Lamentations 3:22-23

God's love never ends, and He always forgives. Every morning I wake up, He is always the same!

—

...For we know how dearly God loves us, because he has given us the Holy Spirit to fill our hearts with his love. Romans 5:5 NLT

God gave me His Holy Spirit to help me know His love.

—

And may you have the power to understand, as all God's people should, how wide, how long, how high, and how deep his love is. Ephesians 3:18 NLT

God wants me to understand just how huge His love is for me.

Every good gift and perfect gift is from above.... James 1:17

Everything that's good comes from God.

—

"For I know the plans I have for you," declares the Lord, "plans to prosper you and not to harm you, plans to give you hope and a future." Jeremiah 29:11 NIV

God has an awesome plan for my life! He will take care of me and has amazing things in store.

—

Taste and see that the Lord is good; blessed is the one who takes refuge in him. Psalm 34:8 NIV

God is good! I can run to Him for help.

GOD KEEPS ME SAFE

God is our Dad, and He is always with us. He watches over us very carefully to keep us safe from harm. Just like we wear helmets when we ride our bikes and learn to look both ways before we cross the street, God tells us in His Word things we can do to avoid accidents and keep ourselves from getting hurt. When people are mean to you or you just don't feel safe, God wants you to call out to Him for help. He will always come running to help you!

Trust in the Lord forever, for the Lord God is an everlasting rock. Isaiah 26:4

God is always going to be here for me. I know I can count on Him.

He tends his flock like a shepherd: He gathers the lambs in his arms and carries them close to his heart.... Isaiah 40:11 NIV

God watches over me with loving care. When I get lost, He brings me safely home.

—

Even when I walk through the darkest valley, I will not be afraid, for you are close beside me. Your rod and your staff protect and comfort me. Psalm 23:4 NLT

Even when scary things happen, I don't have to be afraid because God is with me. He comforts me and keeps me safe.

—

He will cover you with his feathers. He will shelter you with his wings. His faithful promises are your armor and protection. Do not be afraid of the terrors of the night, nor the arrow that flies in the day. Psalm 91:4-5 NLT

God guards me and keeps me safe, like a mamma bird guards her nest. I don't have to be scared during the daytime or when I go to sleep.

—

Though the mountains be shaken and the hills be removed, yet my unfailing love for you will not be shaken nor my covenant of peace be removed," says the Lord, who has compassion on you. Isaiah 54:10

When crazy or scary things happen, God's love and His promises remain the same. He's got me and He cares for me.

—

The name of the Lord is a strong tower; the righteous man runs into it and is safe. Proverbs 18:10

Jesus' name is powerful! I call His name and He keeps me safe.

...If God is for us, who can be against us?
Romans 8:31

It doesn't matter who's against me, because God is on my side.

I CHOOSE TO BE HAPPY

Have you ever had a day when things just didn't go your way? Maybe your friend got picked for the baseball team and you didn't. Maybe your brother took the last piece of pizza when you were hoping for another slice. Or you wish you had cool clothes or a bike like another kid down the street. God wants you to know that He understands—and He wants to help you have a great day anyway!

...Give thanks in all circumstances; for this is the will of God in Christ Jesus for you.
I Thessalonians 5:16-18

I'm glad when things work out for me, and I'm even thankful when they don't...because God wants me to be happy either way!

Do everything without grumbling or arguing. Philippians 2:14 NIV

I do whatever I have to do without arguing or complaining.

—

...Be content with what you have, because God has said, "Never will I leave you; never will I forsake you." Hebrews 13:5 NIV

God is always with me, and that's all I need to be happy.

—

A heart at peace gives life to the body, but envy rots the bones. Proverbs 14:30 NIV

I'm happy with what I have and I'm happy for others too.

—

The lines have fallen for me in pleasant places; indeed, I have a beautiful inheritance. Psalm 16:6

God has given me all that I need and much, much more!

—

All the days of the afflicted are evil, but the cheerful of heart has a continual feast. Proverbs 15:15

Being sad all the time is bad for me. So, I choose to be cheerful!

—

I will offer to you the sacrifice of thanksgiving and call on the name of the Lord. Psalm 116:17

I will tell God why I am thankful. I will tell Him right away!

—

I will give to the Lord the thanks due to His righteousness, and I will sing praise to the name of the Lord, the Most High. Psalm 7:17

I will tell the Lord how good He is. I will sing songs to Him.

Let us come into his presence with thanksgiving; let us make a joyful noise to him with songs of praise! For the Lord is a great God, and a great King above all gods. Psalm 95:2-3

I come to God with a happy heart and celebrate Him by singing because no one is like Him! He's the greatest!

HELP ME!

When you're having a hard time with something, it's really smart to ask for help. It could be that you need help learning a new skill like tying your shoes or casting a fishing rod. Or that the zipper on your backpack got stuck. Sometimes we have way bigger problems than that, but God gave us friends and family to help us. And He will help us too! All we have to do is ask.

God is our refuge and strength, a very present help in trouble. Psalm 46:1

God keeps me safe and strong. If I have trouble with anything, He's right there to help me.

—

...My help comes from the Lord, who made heaven and earth. Psalm 121:2

God made everything I can see—the earth and the stars in the sky. And He is the one who helps me!

—

But the Helper, the Holy Spirit...will teach you all things and bring to your remembrance all that I have said to you. John 14:26

The Holy Spirit teaches me what the Bible says and even helps me remember it at the right times.

—

And David said, "The Lord who delivered me from the paw of the lion and from the paw of the bear will deliver me from the hand of this Philistine...." I Samuel 17:37

God has helped me before, and He will help me again.

—

Trust in the Lord with all your heart, and do not lean on your own understanding. Proverbs 3:5

I trust God with all my heart, and I don't try to do things my own way.

—

Let us then with confidence draw near to the throne of grace, that we may receive mercy and find grace to help in time of need. Hebrews 4:16

I run to God for help. He is kind and forgiving, and He always helps me out.

—

There is no one like the God of Israel. He rides across the heavens to help you, across the skies in majestic splendor. Deuteronomy 33:26 NLT

There's no one else like God—He would cross the whole universe to help me.

—

When the righteous call for help, the Lord hears and delivers them out of all their troubles. Psalm 34:17

I'm God's kid. So, when I need help, He hears me and comes to rescue me.

—

Jesus looked at them and said, "With man this is impossible, but with God all things are possible." Matthew 19:26 NIV

Some things are too hard for me, but nothing is too hard for God.

—

If any of you lacks wisdom, let him ask God, who gives generously to all without reproach, and it will be given him. James 1:5

When I don't know what to do, God wants me to ask Him. He'll show me what to do.

HOW i FEEL

Feelings are funny things. We can be giggly and silly one minute and then sad or mad the next. But no matter what we are feeling, we can be open and honest about it with God. He wants us to know that He understands how we feel and that we don't have to pretend that we are just fine when we really feel bad on the inside. God also wants us to know that we can go to His Word to be comforted and encouraged. He loves to build us up!

Above all else, guard your heart, for everything you do flows from it. Proverbs 4:23 NIV

Above everything and everyone, I trust God with my heart. Then only good stuff will come out of it.

—

Give all your worries and cares to God, for he cares about you. I Peter 5:7 NLT

I can give my worries to God because He cares about me.

—

You have turned my mourning into dancing.... Psalm 30:11

God took away my sadness. Now I'm doing a happy dance!

—

Don't worry about anything; instead, pray about everything. Tell God what you need, and thank him for all he has done. Philippians 4:6 NLT

Instead of worrying, I talk to God about my feelings. I tell Him what I need and I thank Him for what He has already done.

—

A joyful heart is good medicine, but a crushed spirit dries up the bones. Proverbs 17:22

A happy heart makes me feel better. But being in a bad mood takes all my energy away.

Rejoice with those who rejoice, weep with those who weep. Romans 12:15

When someone is happy, I'm happy for them! When someone is sad, I'm sad with them.

—

Why am I discouraged? Why is my heart so sad? I will put my hope in God! I will praise Him again—my Savior and my God! Psalm 42:5-6 NLT

I don't have to be sad or discouraged because I have hope in God. He is awesome!

—

Restore to me the joy of your salvation, and uphold me with a willing spirit. Psalm 51:12

When I lose my joy, God can help me get it back!

HURT FEELINGS

Has someone ever made you feel bad about being you? Maybe they picked on you or didn't include you in a party or a game. Maybe they took something away from you, pushed or hit you, or something even worse. Well, no matter what people say or do to you, God thinks you're special and He loves you just the way you are. He cares about everything that happens to you—and He wants to help you when you're hurting. Here's what God says you should think, say and do when someone bullies you.

See what kind of love the Father has given to us, that we should be called children of God; and so we are. The reason why the world does not know us is that it did not know him. I John 3:1

God loves me and calls me His child—and that's who I am. Those who mistreat me don't know what they're doing...because they don't know God.

...If God is for us, who can be against us? Romans 8:31

It doesn't matter if someone doesn't like me because God is on my side.

—

No weapon that is fashioned against you shall succeed.... Isaiah 54:17

Nothing can wound me. I'm protected by God.

—

"If the world hates you, remember that it hated me first." John 15:18 NLT

Jesus understands how I feel—people weren't very nice to him either.

—

...Weeping may stay for the night, but rejoicing comes in the morning. Psalm 30:5 NIV

Even though things are really hard right now, God is always with me and things will get better!

But God chose what is foolish in the world to shame the wise; God chose what is weak in the world to shame the strong. I Corinthians 1:27

God chose me, and He sees what I can be—even if others seem better than me.

—

And we know that in all things God works for the good of those who love him, who have been called according to his purpose. Romans 8:28 NIV

Everything will work out for my good! God says so.

—

Be strong and courageous. Do not fear or be in dread of them, for it is the Lord your God who goes with you. He will not leave you or forsake you. Deuteronomy 31:6

I am strong and brave. Even when someone is mean to me, I'm not afraid because God is with me—and He's not going anywhere.

Blessed are you when people insult you, persecute you and falsely say all kinds of evil against you because of me. Matthew 5:11 NIV

God takes care of me when people pick on me for believing in Him.

I CAN DO IT!

Sometimes we're given a job that's tough, like when your mom asks you to pick up your toys or clean your room and you just don't feel like helping. But God knows what you are capable of—and you can come to Him for help. When you are tired or frustrated and feel like giving up, ask God to give you a pep talk. If you keep on keeping on with a good attitude, you will be surprised what you can do with God's help.

I can do all things through Him who strengthens me. Philippians 4:13

I can do all things with Jesus' help!

—

...He who is in you is greater than he who is in the world. I John 4:4

God lives in me—and He's stronger than anything.

Whatever your hand finds to do, do it with all your might... Ecclesiastes 9:10 NIV

Whatever job I have to do, I will do it well. I give God my very best.

—

No, in all these things we are more than conquerors through him who loved us. Romans 8:37 NIV

I can tackle anything I need to do because God helps me.

—

But they who wait for the Lord shall renew their strength; they shall mount up with wings like eagles.... Isaiah 40:31

When I get tired, I trust God to give me new strength. He gives me so much that I feel like I can do anything.

—

...I am content with weaknesses, insults, hardships, persecutions, and calamities. For when I

am weak, then I am strong. 2 Corinthians 12:10

It doesn't matter if I feel weak or things seem too hard. I have God to make me strong!

—

Never be lacking in zeal, but keep your spiritual fervor, serving the Lord. Romans 12:11 NIV

I'm excited! I have lots of joy and energy to do what God needs me to do.

—

Count it all joy, my brothers, when you meet trials of various kinds, for you know that the testing of your faith produces steadfastness. And let steadfastness have its full effect, that you may be perfect and complete, lacking in nothing. James 1:2-4

Trouble doesn't slow me down. I keep on moving with God, and He makes me more like Him.

I LOVE GOD!

God is easy to love. He is always here with us—and He has already done so much for us. Sometimes we forget just how good God is. When that happens, it helps to start thinking about the things He's done for us in the past—and to find special ways to say thank you. You can sing Him a song, make some creative artwork, or best of all...you can share His love with someone else!

Bless the Lord, O my soul, and forget not all his benefits. Psalm 103:2

I love God! I'll never forget the good things He's done for me.

—

...We know and rely on the love God has for us. God is love. Whoever lives in love lives in God,

and God in them. I John 4:16 NIV

I know God loves me. God is love. Because He gives me His love, I have plenty to share with others.

—

Jesus replied: "'Love the Lord your God with all your heart and with all your soul and with all your mind.' This is the first and greatest commandment. And the second is like it: 'Love your neighbor as yourself.' Matthew 22:37-39 NIV

I love God with all of me—inside and out. And I treat others the way I want to be treated.

—

Loving God means keeping his commandments, and his commandments are not burdensome. I John 5:3 NLT

I love God and His Word, so it's not too hard to do what's right.

Come, let us worship and bow down. Let us kneel before the Lord our maker, for He is our God.... Psalm 95:6-7 NLT

I sing and shout about how good God is! And I serve Him because He made me.

—

Has the Lord redeemed you? Then speak out! Tell others he has redeemed you from your enemies. Psalm 107:2 NLT

God loves me, and He gave me a brand-new life! I want everyone to know how good He is.

—

**For God has bought you with a great price. So use every part of your body to give glory back to God because he owns it.
I Corinthians 6:20 TLB**

God, I'm all Yours. I'm going to use all my energy, talents and skills for You.

Glorify the Lord with me; let us exalt his name together. Psalm 34:3 NIV

I enjoy celebrating God with my friends and family!

—

Better is one day in your courts than a thousand elsewhere.... Psalm 84:10 NIV

My day is always better when I'm following God.

—

For God so loved the world, that he gave his only Son, that whoever believes in him should not perish but have eternal life. John 3:16

God loves me so much that He gave up His Son, Jesus, for me. He wants me to live with Him in heaven forever. All I have to do is believe Jesus came to save me!

I'M IN GOD'S FAMILY

God chose you to be in His family—and that is so cool! God's family is the best family ever because it's full of all kinds of different people from all over the world. One day we'll all be in heaven together, celebrating all the wonderful things God has done. But we don't have to wait until then to get to know one another. We can help and pray for each other right here, right now!

"I will be a Father to you, and you will be my sons and daughters, says the Lord Almighty." 2 Corinthians 6:18 NIV

God is my Dad, and I am His child.

Therefore be imitators of God, as beloved children. Ephesians 5:1

I want to think and talk and act just like my Dad, God.

—

Even before he made the world, God loved us and chose us in Christ to be holy and without fault in his eyes. Ephesians 1:4 NLT

Even before God made the world, He loved me and picked me to be like Him.

—

Once you were not a people, but now you are God's people; once you had not received mercy, but now you have received mercy. 1 Peter 2:10

I am part of God's family, and He loves me and calls me His kid.

—

God decided in advance to adopt us into his own family by bringing us to himself through Jesus

Christ. This is what he wanted to do, and it gave him great pleasure. Ephesians 1:5 NLT

Because of Jesus, I'm part of God's family.

—

So in Christ we, though many, form one body, and each member belongs to all the others. Romans 12:5 NIV

Just like the different parts of my body, everyone in God's family has a special job to do. It takes all of us working together to finish the job God gave us.

—

There is neither Jew nor Greek, there is neither slave nor free, there is no male and female, for you are all one in Christ Jesus. Galatians 3:28

God's family is made up of all kinds of different people—but we're all the same in His eyes. We are family!

...Jesus called them to him, saying, "Let the children come to me, and do not hinder them, for to such belongs the kingdom of God." Luke 18:16

Jesus loves kids. His kingdom is full of kids like me.

IT'S A GOOD DAY!

Every day is a gift from God—and He wants us to enjoy every minute! Some days are better than others, but no matter what's going on, we can always find our joy in Jesus. When nothing seems to be going right, remember that God is still God and He is always here for you. Ask Him for some help and encouragement, and then trust Him to give it to you. You can start to turn a bad day upside down by reading about how much God loves you in His Word!

The thief comes only to steal and kill and destroy. I came that they may have life and have it abundantly. John 10:10

While the devil wants to give me bad days, Jesus came to save me and give me an amazing life with Him!

These things I have spoken to you, that my joy may be in you, and that your joy may be full. John 15:11

God gives me joy—the kind that never runs out!

—

"...And do not be grieved, for the joy of the Lord is your strength." Nehemiah 8:10

I don't have to be sad. God gave me His joy to make me strong.

—

This is the day that the Lord has made; let us rejoice and be glad in it. Psalm 118:24

God made this day and I'm going to enjoy it and be happy.

—

Rejoice in the Lord always; again I will say, Rejoice. Philippians 4:4

I'm happy because of what God has done for me. I'll say it again: I'm happy!

Let everything that has breath praise the Lord! Praise the Lord! Psalm 150:6

As long as I live, I'll be thankful to God.

—

For You, O Lord, have made me glad by your work; at the works of Your hands I sing for joy. Psalm 92:4

Seeing everything God created makes me so happy I could sing!

—

But thanks be to God, Who in Christ always leads us in triumphal procession, and through us spreads the fragrance of the knowledge of Him everywhere. 2 Corinthians 2:14

I'm thankful for the wonderful ways God leads me. His love makes me like Him. So, people like it when I'm around.

JUST SAY NO!

Have you ever been tempted to do something that you know you shouldn't do? Maybe you gobbled down three cookies when your mom said you could have only two. Or you went to play with friends instead of cleaning up your room. God gives us the freedom to choose what we will do. But He wants us to know that wrong choices bring wrong results, and right choices bring right results. The good news is, with God's help, we can always say no to temptation.

For because he himself has suffered when tempted, he is able to help those who are being tempted. Hebrews 2:18

It's hard to say no to temptation, but Jesus knows how I feel and He's here to help me.

[Jesus] understands our weaknesses, for he faced all of the same testings we do.... Hebrews 4:15 NLT

Sometimes I feel weak, and Jesus gets that. But He kept going and I want to be like Him!

—

...God is faithful, and he will not let you be tempted beyond your ability, but with the temptation he will also provide the way of escape, that you may be able to endure it. I Corinthians 10:13

God never gives me a test I can't pass. When I feel like it's just too hard to do the right thing, I can ask Jesus to help me and He'll show me how to do it.

—

I have stored up your word in my heart, that I might not sin against you. Psalm 119:11

Little by little, I'm learning God's Word so that I can do what it says.

...Walk by the Spirit, and you will not gratify the desires of the flesh. Galatians 5:16

When I'm following God, I don't go my own way; I go His way.

—

God blesses those who patiently endure testing and temptation. Afterward they will receive the crown of life that God has promised to those who love him. James 1:12 NLT

I do what God asks without complaining and He takes good care of me.

—

So humble yourselves before God. Resist the devil, and he will flee from you. James 4:7 NLT

I do what God says and the devil runs away!

Keep watch and pray, so that you will not give in to temptation.... Mark 14:38 NLT

The devil is sneaky, but I know God's voice and I am careful to listen for Him and pray.

LOVING MY FAMILY & FRIENDS

God wants us to be kind and show love to our family and friends. But sometimes getting along with people is hard work. There will be times when you aren't getting along at all, and you don't really want to be loving and patient and kind. But if you ask God to show you how to love your family and friends, you can trust Him to help you. He is always here for you!

Children, obey your parents in the Lord, for this is right. "Honor your father and mother" (this is the first commandment with a promise). Ephesians 6:1-2

I do what my parents tell me and treat them with respect because God asked me to.

Live in harmony with one another.... Romans 12:16

I do my best to get along with others.

—

Submit to one another out of reverence for Christ. Ephesians 5:21 NIV

I put others first because Jesus asks me to.

—

A new commandment I give to you, that you love one another: just as I have loved you, you also are to love one another. John 13:34

I follow Jesus' example to love others the way He has loved me.

—

Greater love has no one than this, that someone lay down his life for his friends. John 15:13

There's no greater way I can show love than to put my friends and family first.

Let all that you do be done in love. I Corinthians 16:14

Whatever I am doing, I do it with love.

—

We love because he first loved us. I John 4:19

I can love others because God loved us first. He taught me how.

—

As iron sharpens iron, so a friend sharpens a friend. Proverbs 27:17 NLT

A true friend will be honest with me and help me to be a better person, and I'll do the same for them.

—

Love is patient and kind; love does not envy or boast; it is not arrogant or rude. It does not insist

on its own way; it is not irritable or resentful.
I Corinthians 13:4-5

I wait patiently for others. I am kind. I am not jealous of others. I am not rude or snobby, and I don't force others to do things my way. I am not grouchy, and I don't stay mad at my family and friends.

OBEYING

Do you remember what that sneaky, old serpent said to Eve in the Garden of Eden? (See Genesis 3:1.) He said, "Did God really say you shouldn't eat from this tree? Its fruit looks so good." He made disobeying God seem like a good thing. He wanted Adam and Eve to break God's rules. That's because Satan hates God and he didn't want Adam and Eve to be friends with God. Well, Satan doesn't want us to be friends with God either. But the truth is, God loves us and if we do what He says, or what our parents and those who love us say, He promises to take care of us.

...The Lord our God we will serve, and his voice we will obey. Joshua 24:24

I listen for God's voice and I do what He says.

For the Lord corrects those he loves, just as a father corrects a child in whom he delights. Proverbs 3:12 NLT

When God shows me that I'm doing something wrong, it's because He loves me - He's my Dad and He's looking out for me.

—

Do not merely listen to the Word...Do what it says. James 1:22 NIV

I don't just listen to God's Word, I do what it says.

—

"You shall have no other gods before me." Deuteronomy 5:7 NIV

In my heart, God always comes first.

—

The Lord will make you the head, not the tail. If you pay attention to the commands of the Lord your God...and carefully follow them, you

will always be at the top, never at the bottom. Deuteronomy 28:13 NIV

God makes me a leader and not a follower because I pay attention to His Word and do what it says.

—

Children, obey your parents in everything, for this pleases the Lord. Colossians 3:20

I obey my parents because it makes God happy.

—

Teach me to do your will, for you are my God.... Psalm 143:10 NIV

God, teach me to follow You and do what You ask.

PATiENCE

Even though it may not always feel like it, waiting is good for us! It gives us a chance to think things over and helps us calm down on the inside, so we don't make hurried decisions. Waiting is a normal, everyday part of life. We wait for green lights when we're driving in the car, for the seasons to change... and for our birthday to finally arrive. And while we are waiting, God wants us to be peaceful. He doesn't want us to feel anxious or to get upset with others. He wants us to enjoy every moment—and with His help, we can! Just remember this: things take time, and God is on your side.

I wait quietly before God, for my victory comes from him. Psalm 62:1 NLT

I never have to yell for God to move faster. I know He's looking out for me.

Therefore the Lord waits to be gracious to you, and therefore he exalts himself to show mercy to you. For the Lord is a God of justice; blessed are all those who wait for him. Isaiah 30:18

God wants to bless me. He's just waiting for the right time.

—

My heart is steadfast, O God, my heart is steadfast! I will sing and make melody! Psalm 57:7

I can sing and be happy while I wait because I know God is working.

—

Whoever is patient has great understanding, but one who is quick-tempered displays folly. Proverbs 14:29 NIV

I am patient with others, and not easily upset.

Put on then, as God's chosen ones, holy and beloved, compassionate hearts, kindness, humility, meekness, and patience, bearing with one another.... Colossians 3:12-13

I am kind, patient and caring. I don't rush ahead of people to get a better spot in line. I slow down to help them!

—

**A hot-tempered person stirs up conflict, but the one who is patient calms a quarrel.
Proverbs 15:18 NIV**

I am calm and patient, and when my friends get upset I help calm them down.

—

Wait for the Lord and keep his way, and he will exalt you to inherit the land.... Psalm 37:34

While I'm waiting, I keep on doing what God says. I know He'll come through.

...Patience is better than pride. Ecclesiastes 7:8 NLT

I'm a patient person. It's okay if I don't get my way.

—

We also pray that you will be strengthened with all his glorious power so you will have all the endurance and patience you need.... Colossians 1:11 NLT

God gives me the strength I need to be patient.

PEACE & QUIET

Did you know that God's peace is amazing? Peace is a calm feeling inside of you that everything is all right. You can have God's peace and stay at rest on the inside because God is with you. And we can also live in peace with one another. God gave you His gift of peace for keeps. So, whether you're playing with your friends or having some quiet time, you can always be at peace. Here's what's really cool: God's peace in you is a sign to others that God lives inside you!

"I am leaving you with a gift—peace of mind and heart.... John 14:27 NLT

God gave me a present—peace to calm my mind and heart.

And let the peace that comes from Christ rule in your hearts.... Colossians 3:15 NLT

The same peace that Jesus has is inside of me!

—

You will keep in perfect peace those whose minds are steadfast, because they trust in you. Isaiah 26:3 NIV

I have lots of peace because I keep God in all my thoughts and I trust Him no matter what.

—

Do not be anxious about anything, but in everything by prayer and supplication with thanksgiving let your requests be made known to God. And the peace of God, which surpasses all understanding, will guard your hearts and your minds in Christ Jesus. Philippians 4:6-7

Instead of getting worried or upset, I talk to God about my feelings. I tell Him what I need, and I thank Him for what He has already done. And He gives me all the peace I need!

...seek peace and pursue it. I Peter 3:11

Wherever God's peace is, that's where I go.

—

And a harvest of righteousness is sown in peace by those who make peace. James 3:18

I plant seeds of peace wherever I go, and God makes them grow.

—

If it is possible, as far as it depends on you, live at peace with everyone. Romans 12:18 NIV

Instead of picking fights, I bring peace instead.

—

So then let us pursue what makes for peace and for mutual upbuilding. Romans 14:19

I try to bring peace and build people up.

Look at those who are honest and good, for a wonderful future awaits those who love peace. Psalm 37:37 NLT

I make friends with people who are honest and good and love peace. A wonderful future awaits us.

—

"Blessed are the peacemakers, for they shall be called sons of God. Matthew 5:9

God calls me His child because I live in peace with others.

—

"Take my yoke upon you and learn from me, for I am gentle and humble in heart, and you will find rest for your souls...." Matthew 11:29-30 NIV

I'm learning to be like Jesus, who is kind and gentle and humble, and it makes me feel peaceful.

PUTTING GOD AND OTHERS FIRST

When Jesus was here on earth, He didn't just live for Himself. He lived to serve His Father in Heaven and all the people on earth. He taught us by example to love others with a selfless love—the kind that puts others first. He loved us so much that He gave His life to give us life. And we can thank God by putting Him and others first.

...It is no longer I who live, but Christ who lives in me. And the life I now live in the flesh I live by faith in the Son of God, who loved me and gave himself for me. Galatians 2:20

I give myself to God completely. He will always be first in my life because He gave His life for me.

The greatest among you shall be your servant. Matthew 23:11

Loving and serving others is the best choice I can make.

—

Don't be selfish; don't try to impress others. Be humble, thinking of others as better than yourselves. Philippians 2:3 NLT

I am not selfish or a show-off. I am more concerned about others than I am about myself.

—

Love one another with brotherly affection. Outdo one another in showing honor. Romans 12:10

I love others like they're my own brothers or sisters. I let them know they're amazing every chance I get.

—

...Serve one another humbly in love. Galatians 5:13 NIV

I simply serve others, with love.

If I then, your Lord and Teacher, have washed your feet, you also ought to wash one another's feet. John 13:14

Jesus volunteered to wash His friends' feet, even though it was a dirty job. I will be like Jesus and serve others too.

—

...He made himself nothing by taking the very nature of a servant.... Philippians 2:7 NIV

Like Jesus, I am here to help others.

—

If anyone forces you to go one mile, go with them two miles. Matthew 5:41 NIV

When someone asks me for help, I do even more for them than what they've asked me to do.

SHARiNG

Sharing with our friends is a good thing. There's always a chance your friend won't share what they have with you, but God wants you to know that you don't ever have to be afraid to share with others. He will always take care of you. And God is more generous than every person put together. The truth is, when you share anything—a hug, a cookie or a game you're playing with—it makes God happy, and it makes you and your friend feel good on the inside too. Sharing is just another way of saying, "I care about you."

Whoever gives to the poor will not want...
Proverbs 28:27

I share what I have with people who need help, and I still have everything I need.

Each one must give as he has decided in his heart, not reluctantly or under compulsion, for God loves a cheerful giver. 2 Corinthians 9:7

When I give something away, I give it with a glad heart. God loves a cheerful giver.

—

Give, and it will be given to you. Good measure, pressed down, shaken together, running over, will be put into your lap...." Luke 6:38

What I give away comes back to me...even more than I gave in the first place.

—

Whatever you give is acceptable if you give it eagerly. And give according to what you have, not what you don't have. 2 Corinthians 8:12 NLT

I am excited to help others, no matter how much I have to give, whether it's a little or a lot.

"...Be on your guard against all kinds of greed; life does not consist in an abundance of possessions." Luke 12:15 NIV

There is more to life than having "stuff." So, I am happy to share what I have.

—

John answered, "Anyone who has two shirts should share with the one who has none, and anyone who has food should do the same." Luke 3:11 NIV

God takes care of me with clothes to wear and food to eat, and I am happy to share them when I see someone in need.

—

..."It is more blessed to give than to receive." Acts 20:35

It's better for me to give than to get.

And he died for all, that those who live should no longer live for themselves but for him who died for them and was raised again.
2 Corinthians 5:15 NIV

Jesus died for me. So, I don't just live for myself. I live to please Him.

TAKING CARE OF MY STUFF

God wants us to take care of our bodies, our homes, our "stuff," our neighborhoods, our world and each other. One way we can honor God is to take care of all the things He's given us. If we prove to be good caretakers of little things, then God will entrust us with bigger things.

The earth is the Lord's, and everything in it.... Psalm 24:1 NLT

Everything I have belongs to God.

—

Lazy hands make for poverty, but diligent hands bring wealth. Proverbs 10:4 NIV

Being lazy won't help me at all, but working hard brings rewards.

—

Every good gift and every perfect gift is from above, coming down from the Father of lights, with whom there is no variation or shadow due to change. James 1:17

Every gift I have comes from God, who doesn't change. He is always the same.

—

"One who is faithful in a very little is also faithful in much"... Luke 16:10

I take good care of what I've been given, and God entrusts me with more.

—

Wealth and honor come from you alone, for you rule over everything.... I Chronicles 29:12 NLT

All my gifts, talents and the things I own come from God. He is in charge of everything.

Precious treasure and oil are in a wise man's dwelling, but a foolish man devours it. Proverbs 21:20

If I spend everything I have today, I won't have anything left for tomorrow.

—

And if you have not been faithful in that which is another's, who will give you that which is your own? Luke 16:12

If I take good care of other people's things, then I can be trusted to have my own things to take care of.

—

She considers a field and buys it; with the fruit of her hands she plants a vineyard. Proverbs 31:16

I use my money wisely, as well as the gifts and talents God gives me.

TALKING TO GOD

Did you know that you can talk to God about anything? Sometimes He'll answer with a really peaceful feeling. Or He'll speak to you in what the Bible calls a "gentle whisper" or a "still, small voice" (see 1 Kings 19:12). God talks to you when you read the Bible and also through the Holy Spirit. He comforts you, helps you figure things out, and stands by to lend you a hand. God is always listening, and He can't wait to hear from you!

The Lord is near to all who call on him, to all who call on him in truth. Psalm 145:18

God is close to me when I pray, and I always tell Him the truth.

—

Never stop praying. 1 Thessalonians 5:17 NLT

I talk to God all the time as I go about my day.

...Ask and you will receive, and your joy will be complete. John 16:24 NIV

I ask God for what I need, and I am full of joy because I know He will help me.

—

And this is the confidence that we have toward him, that if we ask anything according to his will he hears us. I John 5:14

I trust God to answer my prayers in the way that's best for me and He does.

—

So let us come boldly to the throne of our gracious God. There we will receive his mercy, and we will find grace to help us when we need it most. Hebrews 4:16 NLT

I pray to God right away. I know He will forgive me for my sins and help me when I need it most.

"Ask, and it will be given to you; seek, and you will find; knock, and it will be opened to you. For everyone who asks receives, and the one who seeks finds, and to the one who knocks it will be opened. Matthew 7:7-8

I ask God for Help and He helps me. I look for Him and He's there. When I knock on God's door, He always answers.

—

"Again, truly I tell you that if two of you on earth agree about anything they ask for, it will be done for them by my Father in heaven." Matthew 18:19 NIV

When my friends and I get together to pray about something, God goes to work.

—

And the prayer of faith will save the one who is sick, and the Lord will raise him up. And if he has

committed sins, he will be forgiven. James 5:15

My prayers make a difference. When we pray, God heals people who are sick and forgives our sins.

—

I love the Lord, because He has heard my voice and my pleas for mercy. Because He inclined His ear to me, therefore I will call on Him as long as I live. Psalm 116:1-2

I love God because He leans close and hears my voice. I could talk to Him forever.

TELLING THE TRUTH

Have you ever lied to your parents, broken something by accident or done something you knew was wrong...and you wish you could make it better? Well, sometimes accidents happen, and sometimes we even do the wrong thing on purpose. When you mess up, the best thing to do is tell the truth to God and your parents or whoever you need to tell the truth to. God still loves us, and He is always willing to forgive us, no matter what we've done. And the good news is, after we've told the truth, God gives us back His peace and joy...and we feel a lot better on the inside.

So I strive always to keep my conscience clear before God and man. Acts 24:16 NIV

I do my best to keep my heart right and honest.

I am speaking the truth in Christ—I am not lying; my conscience bears me witness in the Holy Spirit. Romans 9:1

I tell the truth, and the Holy Spirit gives me confidence.

—

So set yourselves apart to be holy, for I am the Lord your God. Leviticus 20:7 NLT

I belong to God, so I do what is right.

—

A dishonest man spreads strife, and a whisperer separates close friends. Proverbs 16:28

I don't stir up trouble or whisper lies that ruin my friendships.

—

...If you want to enjoy life and see many happy days, keep your tongue from speaking evil and your lips from telling lies... I Peter 3:10-12 NLT

I want to have a good, long life. So, I think before I speak, and I don't tell lies.

—

If we confess our sins, he is faithful and just to forgive us our sins and to cleanse us from all unrighteousness. If we say we have not sinned, we make him a liar, and his word is not in us.
I John 1:9-10

I talk to God freely about my sins and He always forgives me. But if I say I haven't messed up, then I am not telling the truth.

—

O Lord, who shall sojourn in your tent? Who shall dwell on your holy hill? He who walks blamelessly and does what is right and speaks truth in his heart. Psalm 15:1-2

I do what's right and speak the truth, so I can grow closer to God.

...We will speak the truth in love, growing in every way more and more like Christ, who is the head of his body, the church. Ephesians 4:15 NLT

I tell the truth in love, not just to be right. And I grow more and more like Jesus every day.

—

Keep your tongue from evil and your lips from telling lies. Psalm 34:13 NIV

I don't lie or say hurtful things.

WHAT i SAY

Words come from the heart and they are powerful! So, God wants us to choose our words carefully—to share kind and encouraging comments, loving corrections, useful information and the truth we know from His Word. That way, we will feel good and make others happy with what we say. Sometimes when we're upset, we want to use words to hurt people, but God will always encourage us to tell others that they are loved and special...the way we all want to feel inside!

The Lord God has given me the tongue of those who are taught, that I may know how to sustain with a word him who is weary.... Isaiah 50:4

God gives me wise and encouraging words, so I can make others feel good!

A soft answer turns away wrath, but a harsh word stirs up anger. Proverbs 15:1

My kind words bring peace, but mean words make people angry.

—

Death and life are in the power of the tongue.... Proverbs 18:21

I use my words to encourage people, not cause them harm.

—

Don't use foul or abusive language. Let everything you say be good and helpful, so that your words will be an encouragement to those who hear them. Ephesians 4:29 NLT

I don't use bad words or insults. My words are good and helpful, and they bring encouragement to others.

Kind words are like honey—sweet to the soul and healthy for the body. Proverbs 16:24 NLT

Kind words make me feel better and happy!

—

But now you must put them all away: anger, wrath, malice, slander, and obscene talk from your mouth. Colossians 3:8

I'm finished with all anger and ugly talk.

—

Set a guard over my mouth, Lord; keep watch over the door of my lips. Psalm 141:3 NIV

God helps me watch what I say so I don't hurt others.

—

...the mouth speaks what the heart is full of. A good man brings good things out of the good

stored up in him, and an evil man brings evil things out of the evil stored up in him. Matthew 12:34-35 NIV

Words start inside my heart. A heart filled with good things says words that God says; a heart filled with bad stuff says mean words.

—

...It is wonderful to say the right thing at the right time! Proverbs 15:23 NLT

I am learning to say the right words at the right time.

WHAT IS FAITH?

Faith is believing what God says is true no matter what your thoughts or feelings tell you, and no matter what is happening around you. As God's kids, the most important step of faith we can take is to believe that Jesus is God's Son—and He came to help us! We have faith that God hears us when we pray, that He can make us better when we're sick and for so many other things. Jesus' friend Peter was even able to walk on water because he had faith! (See Matthew 14:22-33.) And if you believe what God says is possible for you—with His help—then you can do the impossible too!

Now faith is confidence in what we hope for and assurance about what we do not see.
Hebrews 11:1 NIV

I know for sure that God will keep His promise, even though my eyes can't see it coming.

So faith comes from hearing, and hearing through the word of Christ. Romans 10:17

My faith comes from hearing God's Word...about everything Jesus did for us.

—

Whoever believes in the Son has eternal life.... John 3:36

Because of my faith in Jesus, I have been given the gift of life with Jesus forever and ever!

—

For it is with your heart that you believe and are justified, and it is with your mouth that you profess your faith and are saved. Romans 10:10 NIV

I know in my heart that Jesus loves me and forgives me, and I tell my friends all about it.

—

For I am not ashamed of the gospel, for it is the power of God for salvation to everyone who believes.... Romans 1:16

I am proud of my faith in Jesus because I believe He saves me.

—

But let him ask in faith, with no doubting, for the one who doubts is like a wave of the sea that is driven and tossed by the wind. James 1:6

I pray without doubting. My faith gives me strength.

—

And the Lord said, "If you had faith like a grain of mustard seed, you could say to this mulberry tree, 'Be uprooted and planted in the sea,' and it would obey you. Luke 17:6

If I have just a little bit of faith, God can do something huge with it.

—

...Whoever believes in me will also do the works that I do; and greater works than these will he

do, because I am going to the Father. John 14:12

I can do amazing things because of my faith in Jesus.

—

..."With man this is impossible, but with God all things are possible." Matthew 19:26

Whatever I can't do, God can!

—

So you see, faith by itself isn't enough. Unless it produces good deeds, it is dead and useless. James 2:17 NLT

Real faith shows. People can see how awesome God is in the things I say and do.

WHAT I THINK ABOUT

Did you know that your thoughts affect your whole life? And did you know that you can choose right now what you are thinking about? Throughout each day, many thoughts come into our heads—good thoughts, silly thoughts, sad thoughts, bad thoughts, mad thoughts. But we can tell each thought that comes our way, "Okay, you can stay" or, "No, you have to go." With God's help, you can make that choice!

O Lord, you have searched me and known me! You know when I sit down and when I rise up; you discern my thoughts from afar. Psalm 139:1-2

God knows everything about me! He knows when I sit down or stand up; He even knows what I'm thinking.

Set your minds on things that are above, not on things that are on earth. Colossians 3:2

I think about all the cool things God is doing around me instead of thinking about things that make me mad or sad.

—

We destroy arguments and every lofty opinion raised against the knowledge of God, and take every thought captive to obey Christ. 2 Corinthians 10:5

I take all my thoughts and give them to God. He shows me what's true.

—

...Be transformed by the renewal of your mind, that by testing you may discern what is the will of God, what is good and acceptable and perfect. Romans 12:2

God's Word teaches me to think like God thinks. It shows me right from wrong and helps me change from the inside out.

For to set the mind on the flesh is death, but to set the mind on the Spirit is life and peace. Romans 8:6

I keep my thoughts on Jesus and it makes me happy!

—

...Let the Spirit renew your thoughts and attitudes. Put on your new nature, created to be like God—truly righteous and holy. Ephesians 4:23-24 NLT

God helps me think about good things and He teaches me to be like Him.

—

Finally, brothers, whatever is true, whatever is honorable, whatever is just, whatever is pure, whatever is lovely, whatever is commendable, if there is any excellence, if there is anything worthy of praise, think about these things. Philippians 4:8

I choose to think about things that make God smile—being kind, telling the truth, loving others.

WHEN I AM SICK

Do you remember how you felt the last time you were sick? Sometimes our body hurts and we don't have much energy, and we have to stay home instead of going to school or playing with friends. But God made us, and He knows how to heal us! He wants you to feel your best in every way! When you feel sick, you can ask God to help you and make you feel better.

Is anyone among you sick? Let him call for the elders of the church, and let them pray over him, anointing him with oil in the name of the Lord. And the prayer of faith will save the one who is sick, and the Lord will raise him up. And if he has committed sins, he will be forgiven.
James 5:14-15

When I am sick, I can ask my family to pray for me in Jesus' name, and God will help me.

The Lord sustains him on his sickbed; in his illness you restore him to full health. Psalm 41:3

God gives me what I need when I am sick. He takes care of me until I'm all better.

—

...By his wounds you have been healed. I Peter 2:24

Jesus was hurt so that I could be healed!

—

...Listen carefully to my words. Don't lose sight of them. Let them penetrate deep into your heart, for they bring life to those who find them, and healing to their whole body.
Proverbs 4:20-22 NLT

I listen carefully to the words of Jesus. They go to work in my heart and make my whole body healthy.

—

"You must serve only the Lord your God. If you do, I will bless you with food and water, and I will

protect you from illness. Exodus 23:25 NLT

I listen to God, and He takes care of the water I drink and the food I eat. He protects me from getting sick.

—

He sent out his word and healed them, and delivered them from their destruction. Let them thank the Lord for his steadfast love, for his wondrous works to the children of man! Psalm 107:20-21

God sent His Son, Jesus, to heal me and forgive me when I sin. I am thankful for His love and the good things He has done!

—

Bless the Lord, O my soul, and forget not all his benefits, who forgives all your iniquity, who heals all your diseases, who redeems your life from the pit, who crowns you with steadfast love and mercy. Psalm 103:2-4

God's always taking care of me! He forgives me, makes me feel better when I'm sick, and loves me so much!

—

O Lord my God, I cried to you for help, and you have healed me. Psalm 30:2

I cry to God for help and He heals me.

WHEN I'M MAD

Remember the last time you or someone you know was mad? How did it make you feel? God wants us to know it's okay to feel mad, but He doesn't want us to act out in ways that hurt others. The truth is, it doesn't do us any good when our feelings get out of control, God can help us get back in control. You can talk to God about what happened and trust Him to work everything out.

Beloved, never avenge yourselves, but leave it to the wrath of God, for it is written, "Vengeance is mine, I will repay, says the Lord." Romans 12:19

I don't try to get even with people who hurt me. I leave it in God's hands, because He promises to make things right.

But I say to you, Love your enemies and pray for those who persecute you. Matthew 5:44

I love everyone—even people who don't like me. And I pray for people who hurt me.

—

...Do not lose your temper—it only leads to harm. Psalm 37:8 NLT

I control my anger. If I don't, it only ends up hurting others.

—

Be angry and do not sin; do not let the sun go down on your anger. Ephesians 4:26

When I'm angry, I don't act out. And I make peace with others before bedtime.

—

Good sense makes one slow to anger, and it is his glory to overlook an offense. Proverbs 19:11

It doesn't make sense to get angry quickly. And it's good for me to forgive others instead of getting mad.

Do not be overcome by evil, but overcome evil with good. Romans 12:21

I don't let bad things get to me. I trust God and do good no matter how I feel.

—

A hot-tempered person stirs up conflict, but the one who is patient calms a quarrel. Proverbs 15:18 NIV

I don't get mad and start fights. I stay calm and bring peace where there is fighting.

—

...Let every person be quick to hear, slow to speak, slow to anger. James 1:19

I listen first, think before I speak, and I don't get angry.

WHEN WE'RE LONELY

There are so many reasons why we get lonely. Maybe your best friend moved away. Or you're the new kid in class and you're having a hard time making friends. Maybe you feel alone when you come home or wish you could join in after-school activities. God wants you to know that He's your forever friend and you can count on Him to comfort you when you're lonely. He can even help you find a brand-new friend!

I love all who love me. Those who search will surely find me. Proverbs 8:17 NLT

God loves me and is always near me. I always find Him when I look for Him.

...Abide in my love. John 15:9

I wrap God's love around me like a cozy blanket.

—

Because of your unfailing love, I can enter your house.... Psalm 5:7 NLT

Because God loves me more than anything, I can come to Him any time.

—

..."Behold, I am with you always, to the end of the age." Matthew 28:20

God will always be with me. Always.

—

He comforts us in all our troubles so that we can comfort others. When they are troubled, we will be able to give them the same comfort God has given us. 2 Corinthians 1:4 NLT

God comforts me when I'm having a hard time. So, when someone else is going through something tough, I will know how to make them feel better too.

—

For my father and my mother have forsaken me, but the Lord will take me in. Psalm 27:10

Even if people who are close to me turn away from me, God will always take me in.

—

"I will not leave you as orphans; I will come to you." John 14:18

God will never leave me all alone. He will always be there for me.

—

Draw near to God, and he will draw near to you.... James 4:8

I get closer and closer to God, and He comes closer to me.

WHO JESUS MADE ME TO BE

God made you special—and He has a special plan for your life! He wants you to know how precious you are in His eyes, even if sometimes you may not see what He sees. The truth is, you're so valuable to God that He sent His only Son, Jesus, to give you life with Him forever! He wants you to love the amazing person He created you to be, and to join Him in every wonderful adventure He's planned just for you.

For we are God's handiwork, created in Christ Jesus to do good works, which God prepared in advance for us to do. Ephesians 2:10 NIV

God made me Himself. He created me to be like Jesus and help others. He has great things planned for me to do!

Therefore, if anyone is in Christ, the new creation has come: The old has gone, the new is here! 2 Corinthians 5:17 NIV

When I gave my life to Jesus, I became brand new! The old me went away and the new me is here!

—

The Spirit himself bears witness with our spirit that we are children of God. Romans 8:16

The Holy Spirit tells me that I am a child of God.

—

...God loved us and chose us in Christ to be holy and without fault in his eyes. Ephesians 1:4 NLT

God loved me and chose me to be His child, and when He looks at me, He is so happy!

—

...You are a chosen race, a royal priesthood, a holy nation, a people for his own possession, that you may proclaim the excellencies of him who

called you out of darkness into his marvelous light. I Peter 2:9

I am one of God's chosen kids. My job is to tell others about how awesome He is!

—

"Before I formed you in the womb I knew you, and before you were born I consecrated you; I appointed you a prophet to the nations." Jeremiah 1:5

God knew me before I was a baby. He chose me to be His messenger to the world.

—

I praise you, for I am fearfully and wonderfully made. Wonderful are your works; my soul knows it very well. Psalm 139:14

God made me special and I am one of a kind. Everything He does is good!

ISBN : 978-1-942854-95-1

Joyce Meyer Ministries
P.O. Box 655
Fenton, Missouri 63026
joycemeyer.org